A PRACTICAL GUIDE
TO LEGAL ISSUES
AFFECTING
COLLEGE TEACHERS

By Patricia A. Hollander,
    D. Parker Young,
    Donald D. Gehring

The Higher Education Administration Series
Edited by Donald D. Gehring and D. Parker Young

COLLEGE ADMINISTRATION PUBLICATIONS, INC.

This monograph is a part of
The Higher Education Administration Series
which also includes:
☐ Administering College and University Housing:
   A Legal Perspective
☐ The Dismissal of Students with Mental Disorders:
   Legal Issues, Policy Considerations, and
   Alternative Responses

College Administration Publications, Inc.,
P. O. Box 8492, Asheville, N. C. 28814

© 1985 College Administration Publications, Inc.,
All rights reserved. Published 1985
Printed in the United States of America
90 89 88 87   5 4 3 2

Library of Congress Cataloging in Publication Data

Hollander, Patricia A.
    A practical guide to legal issues affecting college
teachers.

    (The higher education administration series)
    1. College teachers—Legal status, laws, etc.—United
States.   I. Young, D. Parker (Douglas Parker),
1933-   II. Gehring, Donald D.   III. Title.
IV. Series.
KF4240.H65   1985   344.73'078   85-16644
ISBN 0-912557-02-8   347.30478

The views expressed in this book are those of the individual authors
and are not necessarily those of College Administration Publications,
Inc.

This publication is designed to provide accurate and authoritative information in regard to the subject matter covered. It is sold with the
understanding that the publisher is not engaged in rendering legal, accounting or other professional service. If legal advice or other expert
assistance is required, the services of a competent professional person
should be sought.
*—from a Declaration of Principles jointly adopted by a committee of the
American Bar Association and a committee of publishers.*

ii

Table of Contents

Foreword

Our society is becoming more and more litigious. As this trend continues, every segment of our culture is subject to legal attack. Faculty who once held a preferred position in our social structure are no longer safe from lawsuits. The amount of case law involving faculty is rising in proportion to the general increase in litigation. Most of the suits involving faculty can be attributed to the relationships faculty have as teachers with their students and their institutions.

Students who now enter our nation's colleges and universities come to gain an economic advantage. Postsecondary education is seen as utilitarian and students have a very egocentric orientation. The rising admission standards of graduate and professional schools place extreme presure on students to achieve the highest possible grades. Business, industry and professional firms are also more often interested in only the top students. Often in striving for the highest grades students are places in competition with each other. The pressure is tremendous!

The pressure for grades explodes into lawsuits when students believe they have been treated unfairly, had their rights abridged or have been discriminated against by those who hold the power of the grade: the faculty. Through their teaching and advising activities faculty are at the very core of the credentialing process. Students are much better consumers today and will not hesitate to challenge faculty to ensure they are getting what they paid for.

These social trends—increased litigation, grade pressure, consumerism and the demise of any faculty mystique—have made it clear that faculty must be exposed to their legal rights and responsibilities as teachers. The authors of this monograph have provided a very practical guide to help faculty understand their legal relationship to students and to the institutions they serve. Understanding those relationships then leads to an understanding of the rights and responsibilities of each party—students, faculty and the institutions.

This monograph is written by faculty for faculty. While the authors have extensive experience in college law, they have written for the lay reader. There is no legal jargon but simple practical everyday language addressing common faculty problems. The information presents a very concise review of the most up-to-date case law related to college teaching. The authors, however, have elected to omit specific case references in order to facilitate readability. The checklist provides practical assistance to the college teacher.

This monograph will be of value to deans, department chairs and individual faculty. While others may profit from its use, it has been specifically prepared for college and university teachers with the purpose of increasing knowledge and decreasing litigation.

DDG
DPY
July 1985

About the Authors

PATRICIA A. HOLLANDER is an attorney in Buffalo, New York. Since 1972 she has been the General Counsel of the American Association of University Administrators, and has consulted extensively in the fields of education and computer law. She also speaks before many educational and legal groups.

Ms. Hollander received her J.D. law degree from St. Louis University and did graduate work at Harvard Law School. At the State University of New York at Buffalo, she served for almost a decade as both an administrator and a faculty member in the School of Management and in the School of Law. In spring 1980, she taught at the University of Virginia's Center for the Study of Higher Education, as Visiting Professor.

Ms. Hollander is the author of *Legal Handbook for Educators*, published in 1978. She is co-author with John Pine of *The Public Administrator and the Courts*, to be published in 1985. Since its inception in 1983, she has been an editor of *The Computer Law Monitor*, a quarterly publication that summarizes in lay language significant court cases concerning computer technology.

Among her recent writings is the chapter, "University Computing Facilities: Some Ethical Dilemmas," she contributed to Baca and Stein's 1983 book, *Ethical Principles, Problems, and Practices in Higher Education*. Her article, "An Introduction to Legal and Ethical Issues Relating to Computers in Higher Education," appeared in the fall 1984 issue of the *Journal of College and University Law*. Also in 1984, her chapter, "The Chief Student Affairs Officer as Employer and Manager: A Special Risk," appeared in Owens' June 1984 book, *Risk Management and The Student Affairs Professional*, in the NASPA Monograph Series.

Her latest book, *Computers In Education: Legal Liabilities and Ethical Issues Concerning Their Use and Misuse*, will be published in fall 1985.

DR. D. PARKER YOUNG is Professor of Higher Education and Graduate Coordinator in the Institute of Higher Education at the University of Georgia. Dr. Young serves as Vice President of the National Organization on Legal Problems of Education. He has served on the Board of Directors of NOLPE as well as the American Association of University Administrators. Dr. Young, along with Dr. Gehring received the National Association of Student Personnel Administrator's 1985 Award for Outstanding Contribution to Literature or Research. He has authored many books, such as *The Yearbook of Higher Education Law*, monographs, articles and other publications in the area of higher education law. He is a contributing and consulting editor for several publications including *The College Student and the Courts, The College Administrator and the Courts, The Schools and the Courts*, and *The Computer Law Monitor*. He also writes a continuing column on legal issues for the National Association of Academic Affairs Newsletter. Dr. Young has been invited to address numerous higher education organizations and groups on the topic of legal issues in higher education.

DR. DONALD D. GEHRING is a Professor of Higher Education and a member of the Graduate Faculty of the University of Louisville. He also serves as the University Student Grievance Officer. Dr. Gehring received the School of Education Distinguished Teaching Award in 1982 and with Dr. Young received the National Association of Student Personnel Administrator's 1985 Award for Outstanding Contribution to Literature or Research. He serves on the Editorial Board of NOLPE, NASPA and SACSA. He is a member of the Board of Directors of the National Center for the Study of the College Fraternity. He has published a variety of journal articles, books, chapters, videotapes and monographs. His publications include such topics as "Legal Issues Related to Academic Advising," "The Mandatory Withdrawal of Students with Mental Disorders" and "Academic Integrity: Legal Issues and Policy Considerations." Dr. Gehring has served as a consultant to institutions throughout the United States and Puerto Rico and has presented national workshops for faculty and administrators.

Chapter 1

Introduction

This is a practical guide for college teachers, outlining the principal legal issues related to their teaching duties in the classroom. The guide stresses the legal rights and responsibilities of college teachers in their relationship with their students and their employers. Some of these legal responsibilities arise from statutes, student enrollment contracts, teacher employment contracts, and the legal duty of reasonable care under the circumstances. At public colleges, additional legal responsibilities arise from the U.S. Constitution and from the constitutions of the states.

The responsibilities and rights of college teachers and students, very briefly stated, are as follows. The college teacher has the responsibility of providing academically sound teaching (in some cases research and service activities as well) along with appropriate behavior as set forth in the college catalogue and in his or her employment contract; and has a right to salary and promotions as agreed. The college student has the responsibility of meeting academic, behavior and financial standards; and has a right to receive a degree.

The days are long past when a college teacher had to pay little or no attention to the possibility of being sued in connection with being employed to teach. Courts routinely are asked to resolve conflicts related to college education, including those between college students and their teachers and colleges, between college teachers and their colleges and students, and even between colleges themselves.

College teachers have been sued for many reasons, such as failing to teach a course as described in a college catalogue, not attending class regularly, failing to provide proper instruction and supervision in a laboratory, shop, or physical education class, allegedly defaming students, and for discrimination based on race or sex. This list could be expanded greatly since we do live in a litigious society

1

and court cases have been filed where college teachers are named as defendants in almost ever conceivable area of college life.

The one area in which courts are reluctant to act is that requiring academic judgment, such as decisions about what grade a student deserves or whether a student has met course requirements academically. Although historically courts have been reluctant to hear such cases they have been willing to act in cases where a teacher was said to grade in an arbitrary, capricious, or malicious fashion, as where almost all students in a class were given failing grades.

This guide is meant to help make college teachers aware of current legal parameters so that they do not get either themselves or their institutions in legal trouble.

Chapter II

Legal Relationships

LEGAL RELATIONSHIPS BETWEEN STUDENTS AND THEIR INSTITUTIONS

Former In Loco Parentis Relationship

Formerly, the relationship between a college student and a college was treated much as a traditional parent-child relationship. Today it is clear that the relationship has changed. No longer is an institution or college professor presumed always to know what is best for the student. Nor is a student expected to accept without question whatever directives and rules the institution or teacher issues.

In the past, a student certainly was accountable to the college, but it was not at all clear that a college or a college teacher was accountable to the student. Today, there is legal accountability on all sides.

Contractual Relationship

Today, courts recognize that when a student pays tuition for a college education, a legal contract comes into being. The student has contracted for an education as advertised by the institution in its catalog and by its representatives. Some like to think of the student as a consumer of education, and an institution as a supplier of a product called education. The consumer is entitled to receive what was paid for. The old days of in loco parentis have been replaced by the law of contracts and the concepts of consumerism. This contractual relationship implies a property interest which also triggers constitutional guarantees at public institutions.

Constitutional Relationship

Students who attend public institutions find that they have certain constitutional rights in addition to contractual rights. Constitutional rights arise from the fact that public institutions are "arms of the state." Thus, the actions of a public college and its officials are actions of the state. Students at public colleges are protected by the federal and states' constitutions against certain "state action." For instance, public college students are protected by the First Amendment from state actions that interfere with the right to free expression, as in the publication of student newspapers. Public college students also are protected by the Fourteenth Amendment from state actions that interfere with the right of due process, as in being expelled for misconduct without a hearing.

On the other hand, students who attend private colleges are not so protected because private colleges are not "arms of the state." The actions of private colleges are private actions, not public actions. The principal protection of private college students rests with their contract of enrollment.

LEGAL RELATIONSHIP BETWEEN TEACHER AND INSTITUTION

A legal contract of employment exists between a college teacher and the employing institution. A teacher is expected to perform whatever duties are set forth in the employment contract and the institution is expected to pay salaries and fringe benefits as agreed. A failure by either party to fulfill the agreed upon obligations may result in a suit alleging breach of contract.

A college teacher generally would be indemnified by the employing institution for awards of damages resulting from a lawsuit so long as the teacher was acting within the scope of employment. However, where the teacher was acting outside the scope of employment, the institution may not provide a defense or indemnification. Examples of acts found to be outside the scope of employment have included racial slurs, sexual harassment, and assault and battery.

Teachers at public institutions, like students at public institutions, have certain rights protected by the federal or state constitutions. No one can be punished just because he or she exercises a basic right which the individual already has. Thus, a public college teacher has First Amendment free expression rights and may not be terminated for writing to the local newspaper and expressing an opinion in opposition to that of the college so long as the subject matter is of public concern. A college teacher also has Fourteenth Amendment due process and equal protection rights.

LEGAL RELATIONSHIP BETWEEN TEACHER AND STUDENT

Teacher As Agent of Institution

When a teacher is acting within the scope of his or her employment, a teacher generally is viewed as the agent of the institution. A teacher's acts, then, are considered to be the acts of the institution.

Thus, a teacher's acts can form the basis for liability of the institution. For example, if a teacher of history refuses to follow the syllabus for a history course and insists on teaching more writing skills than history in the course, a dissatisfied student may sue the institution as well as the teacher for breach of contract of enrollment. Also, where a biology teacher takes a class on a field trip and a student is injured during the trip, then both the institution and the teacher may be named as defendants.

Teacher As Exemplar

A teacher also serves as a role model or exemplar for students. Thus, a student has the right to expect that a teacher will set a good example as to intellectual rigor and honesty, will give attribution credits to students whose work is used by the teacher, and be willing to spend a reasonable amount of time familiarizing students with the mores and standards of the academic world.

A student also has a right to expect that a college teacher will be qualified and legitimate. A substantial failure by an institution to check a teacher's credentials and teaching behavior may expose the institution as well as the teacher to liability for breach of the contract of enrollment and/or for fraud.

Teacher's Acts Outside the Scope of Employment

Certain acts of a teacher may be considered to be outside the scope of the teacher's employment, so as to expose the teacher individually to liability, but not the institution. If a teacher wrongfully were to collect fees from students in exchange for a password providing access to a college computer, but the college knew nothing of the practice, the college would take the position that the teacher was acting outside the scope of employment and the college would seek to avoid liability. The teacher may, however, be liable to the students and to the college, and in addition, may be liable to criminal prosecution. In other words, where a teacher's actions are not part of the regular employment duties, the teacher alone may be liable.

SOURCES OF LEGAL RIGHTS AND RESPONSIBILITIES AT PUBLIC AND PRIVATE COLLEGES

A list of basic sources of legal rights and responsibilities at colleges would include the following:

Constitutions

(Federal and State) — at public colleges only.

For example, the First Amendment of the U.S. Constitution refers to deprivations by public officials of a person's freedom of expression, press, association, and religion. The Fourth Amendment refers to freedom from unreasonable searches and seizures without search warrants. The Fourteenth Amendment refers to freedom from deprivation of liberty (good name and reputation) and property (attending college) without due process. The Fourteenth Amendment also refers to equal protection under the law. That is, prohibition against arbitrary classifications such as not allowing a student to attend class because the student has long hair, to the dislike of the teacher.

Statutes

(Federal and State)—Examples would be statutes prohibiting discrimination based on race, national origin, religion, sex, age, and handicap; or state administrative statutes.

Contracts

These would include students' contracts of enrollment, employees' contracts covering terms and conditions of employment, and contracts for various goods and services.

Policies of Governing Boards

Policies of a board of trustees or board of regents usually set forth the mission of the college, student admission and graduation policies, and personnel policies. These policies become implicit and often explicit terms of the teacher's contract or the student's enrollment contract.

Handbooks

Student, faculty, staff and other handbooks contain the more detailed rules and regulations that implement the basic policies set by the governing board. These rules and regulations also become part of the contracts relating to teachers and students.

Professional Standards

Examples of these would be the standards of the American Association of University Professors (AAUP), the American Association of University Administrators (AAUA), and the National Association of Student Personnel Administrators (NASPA).

Custom and Traditions

Under certain circumstances, longstanding and widely accepted traditions at a college may form the basis for legal rights. For instance, at some colleges that do not recognize officially the AAUP time limits for notice of faculty terminations, a tradition of providing that some timely notice has been followed routinely for many years, so that if one faculty member suddenly does not receive such notice, the faculty member may claim a "right" to that notice. Also, where an institution has a tradition of allowing all students to take a re-exam, then a particular student cannot be refused a request for such.

Duty of Reasonable Care Under the Circumstances

Where a duty of reasonable care exists, has been breached, an injury results from that breach, and there are damages, a legal basis for a claim of negligence may be made.

6

Chapter III

Legal Distinction Between Public and Private Colleges

STATE ACTION—CONSTITUTIONAL PROTECTIONS

At public colleges there exist certain constitutional rights. A public college is considered to be an "arm of the state." The actions of its teachers, staff, and administrators are considered to be state actions. The federal and state constitutions protect individuals against certain state actions. Among these are deprivation of freedom of expression, press, association, and religion (First Amendment), as well as deprivation of due process and equal treatment under the law (Fourteenth Amendment). Thus, students, faculty, staff, and administrators at public colleges have constitutional rights that must be protected. When these rights are breached, legal action often results.

Although it occurs rarely, a private institution may be found to be engaged in "state action" if it is so entwined with the state to the extent that the state is actually involved in the governance of the institution.

CONTRACTUAL RELATIONSHIP: PRIVATE COLLEGES

At private colleges, most legal rights are based on contractual relationships. In the case of students, the contractual relationship is based on a contract of enrollment. In the case of faculty, staff, and administrators, the contractual relationship is based on a contract of employment.

CONTRACTUAL RELATIONSHIP: PUBLIC COLLEGES

It must be emphasized that contractual relationships exist also in public colleges, just as they do in private colleges. The major difference between private and public colleges is that public colleges have both contractual and constitutional relationships.

7

Chapter IV

Academic Affairs

CONTRACTUAL ACADEMIC REQUIREMENTS TO EARN A DEGREE

At both public and private institutions, the academic requirements needed to obtain a degree are a part of the contract of enrollment between the student and the institution. An institution is expected to set forth clearly its degree requirements, and students are expected to meet them. When an institution determines that a student has failed academically, courts tend to refuse to review or otherwise intrude on that decision on the ground that courts have no academic expertise. There are exceptions to this general rule, as when a court finds that an institution has acted in an arbitrary or capricious fashion. Normally, however, courts will not intrude in decisions regarding required courses, grading, and other academic criteria. However, there are cases where institutions have been ordered to grant degrees as well as a grade when a student has been exonerated of academic dishonesty charges, or where the institution or an individual teacher failed to follow prescribed procedures.

It is incumbent on an institution to be sure that the catalogue sets forth accurately all academic requirements. Course descriptions should be accurate and reflect what is actually taught.

Faculty members should provide students with a syllabus at the outset of a course, and follow it within reason. Students should be told at the beginning of a course just what the policy is regarding such things as absences and tardiness. Faculty members also have an obligation to be well informed about the subject matter of the course, to be reasonably up to date, to hold reasonable office hours, to grade objectively and fairly, and to be reasonably accommodating to emergencies in students' lives. Faculty should not be arbitrary and capricious, such as a week before a spring break changing the due date for

9

a long paper from the day after the break to the day before the break. Teachers certainly should stick to the subject matter and not spend an inordinate amount of class time on topics not related to the subject. For example, students may object to paying for a course in which the professor's political views take up a significant portion of time.

ADMISSIONS

Admissions criteria should be set forth clearly in the catalogue, and the institution should assess applications for admissions according to the criteria and without discrimination. Both subjective and objective criteria may be used in making the admission decision so long as the criteria are relevant and not discriminatory.

ACADEMIC ADVISING

When college teachers serve as academic advisors, they should be fully informed as to all requirements for securing a degree. Inaccurate advising may involve institutional liability. It is unwise for faculty members to offer casual academic advice. Students with questions should be directed to persons designated by the institution to give academic advice.

CHANGING ACADEMIC REQUIREMENTS

Academic requirements may be changed from time to time to reflect new developments in disciplines. Students must meet the new requirements, but should be accommodated to the extent possible in doing so. Sometimes a grace period, or "grandfathering," is provided as a transition to new academic requirements.

GRADING

Faculty should inform students at the outset of a course about how grades will be calculated, i.e., what tests, papers, or other requirements will be used. Teachers may use both objective as well as subjective criteria in grading. However, students should be told of these criteria and how they will be weighted. Grades should be turned in by faculty in a timely fashion.

ACADEMIC DISHONESTY (Cheating and Plagiarism)

Historically, academic dishonesty has been treated as a breach of academic requirements with little opportunity for due process to be afforded the accused student. Recent court decisions, however, increasingly equate academic dishonesty with infractions of the disciplinary code. Courts now refer to a "liberty interest" of students whenever they are accused of academic dishonesty. This is because an accused student's good name, reputation, and integrity are brought into question. Since students in public institutions are protected by the Fourteenth Amendment guarantee against a deprivation of a liberty interest, an accused student should be afforded some measure of due process. Private institutions must follow whatever rules regarding academic dishonesty are set forth in their contracts of enrollment.

ACADEMIC DUE PROCESS

Academic due process generally involves substantive due process, that is, determining academic competence by evaluating academic criteria. In strictly academic affairs there is no absolute right to procedural due process, that is providing notice and hearing before a suspension or dismissal based on academic failure. The adoption of grievance procedures provides an excellent opportunity to resolve many disputes in the academic arena. Exhaustion of all administrative remedies must usually be completed before a court will hear a dispute.

Chapter V

Student Rights and Responsibilities

Although college teachers usually do not have direct responsibility in the area of student affairs, they must have an appreciation of student rights and responsibilities. This allows the teacher to understand why students must be treated in certain ways in order that legal parameters are respected.

Student rights and responsibilities at public institutions are different from those at private institutions. The principal difference is that public institutions are held to the constitutional standards required of state entities. Private institutions are not. Thus, college teachers at public institutions must take into account constitutional requirements, such as due process or freedom of expression when decisions are made about student activities.

College teachers at both public and private institutions also need to be aware of three principal sets of requirements regarding student activities. These are the requirements of the contract of enrollment between the student and the college, requirements of applicable state and federal statutes, and general requirements of reasonable supervision to avoid claims of negligence.

FREEDOM OF EXPRESSION

College teachers at public institutions would do well to remember that their students have protected First Amendment constitutional rights to free expression. Students have a right, for instance, to state their views on political issues. The institution has a right, on the other hand, to reasonably regulate this expression as to time, place, and manner of expression so as to prevent disruption of the educational process or interference with the rights of others, and prevent placing persons or property in danger.

Students at public institutions, then, may speak their minds at a designated "speaker's corner" on campus. However, they may not disrupt the educational process by insisting they have a right to use time in class to state their political views. The same may be said with regard to so-called commercial speech, that is, speech concerned with advertising or selling products. On the other hand, if a college is going to be a free marketplace of ideas, college teachers should permit students to engage in relevant scholarly expression in class, even if it means hearing unpopular views.

Private institutions may regulate free expression of students simply by making clear rules as to what expression by students will be permitted, and then following those rules. Students will be expected to obey the rules or suffer the sanctions provided in the rules.

STUDENT PUBLICATIONS

Students at public institutions are protected by the First Amendment right of free press. Student newspapers at public institutions generally cannot be censored prior to publication. Student editors usually are permitted to publish and take the risk of allegations of libel or obscenity. The student press at public institutions is subject to restriction only where college officials can "reasonably forecast substantial disruption or material interference" with educational activities, or that the material is clearly libelous or obscene.

At private institutions where the college supplies financial support for the student newspaper, the college is deemed to be the publisher of the paper and may be liable for what is printed in it. A private college-publisher may set up a system of prior review of student publications to monitor for libel, obscenity, or other matters of possible legal liability.

Some private colleges supply no financial support to student publications, which then are deemed to be independent. The college may be protected from suits in such situations, although some legal authorities take the view that a private college has an inherent right to control student publications and therefore has some exposure to liability, whether the control is exercised or not.

STUDENT ORGANIZATIONS

At public institutions, students have a First Amendment right of free association. In recent years some public colleges have attempted, unsuccessfully, to refuse to recognize certain student organizations, such as student homosexual clubs. Public institutions which allow for recognition of organizations may not refuse recognition unless the group is dedicated to disruption or violence or other unlawful activities or that it would incite others to engage in such activity or that it refuses to agree in advance to abide by reasonable rules and regulations.

At private institutions, student organizations may be regulated by policies set forth by the institution. These policies may be treated as part of the contract of enrollment between the student and the institution. Thus, student homosexual clubs may be prohibited at private institutions.

SEPARATION OF CHURCH AND STATE

The First Amendment prohibits the establishment of any religion by the government, and provides for the free exercise of religious beliefs. At public institutions, courts have refused to permit any aid to religion. Such practices as a teacher reading from the Bible and having a prayer during class is prohibited. Religious clubs and organizations may be permitted on the same basis as other student clubs.

At private institutions there is no constitutional restriction rules regarding religious activities by students.

SEARCH AND SEIZURE

Students, as any other citizen, are protected by the Fourth Amendment to the United States Constitution against unreasonable searches and seizures. If, however, there is "reasonable cause to believe" that a criminal law is being violated or that harm or danger is present, a search on campus may be considered reasonable.

Teachers and administrators at public institutions generally are considered to be public officials, so, in most instances, they should search only with a warrant. Under emergency conditions, a search without a warrant possibly would be permitted. Where a student enters a classroom wearing what appears to be a gun or knife, a teacher may request the student to remove them and empty pockets or purse; and if the student refuses, the teacher should send the student out of the classroom or seek assistance from the campus security guards. However, the teacher may not require a student to open a briefcase or purse, etc., simply because the teacher is suspicious of illegal drugs or other contraband.

Although on the private campus the Fourth Amendment may not apply, it is wise not to arbitrarily conduct searches since everyone has an inherent right of privacy.

DUE PROCESS

Students at public institutions may have two rights to due process, a constitutional right under the Fourteenth Amendment, and a contractual right under the student's contract of enrollment with the institution. At private institutions, students have only whatever contractual right to due process exists by virtue of the terms of the student's contract of enrollment with the institution.

The Fourteenth Amendment requires due process before a governmental entity, such as a public institution, may deprive one of life, liberty, or property. In a college setting, a student's good name and reputation are considered a "liberty" right, and a student's right to attend college is considered a "property" right. Due process would be required before a student is deprived of either at a public institution. A college teacher should not place a stigma on a student's good name without hearing the student's defense.

There are two kinds of due process, substantive and procedural. Substantive due process requires, essentially, that policies and rules must be related to the basic government purpose at hand and that basic fairness be employed. For instance, college rules should be related to educational matters and applied fairly. Procedural due process generally refers to the requirement for notice and hearing before being deprived of a right. For example, before being expelled for misconduct, students should have notice of what they have done wrong and a chance to tell their side of the story.

Due process may be very simple in form. The notice and hearing may consist of the dean's telling a student what the charge is, and merely hearing what the student has to say about the matter. However, the more serious the possible penalty is, the more formal the notice and hearing should be.

EQUAL PROTECTION OF THE LAW

Students at public institutions have a right, under the Fourteenth Amendment, to equal protection under the law. Thus, all students at public institutions must be treated equally under the college's rules. For instance, if some students are allowed to graduate without meeting certain requirements, other students should have the opportunity to show they should be granted the same dispensation. Teachers may not treat some students differently than others without some valid justification. For example, students who wore T-shirts to class could not be given an extra assignment not given to the other students in the class.

The constitutional right to equal protection does not apply to students at private institutions. However, as a matter of equity and good practice, a private institution usually treats students equally. This requirement at a private institution may take the form of a written policy or may be a matter of general tradition and practice.

Dress Codes

Dress codes are rare at public institutions. Certainly, a public institution would be concerned about modes of dress that posed issues of health and safety. If, for example, wearing knives or guns became fashionable, a public institution would be on firm legal ground in prohibiting that mode of dress. In general, the only dress code which a teacher could enforce would be one which prohibited dress or appear-

16

ance which would cause disruption. For example, a teacher certainly may prohibit students from wearing costumes to class that would disrupt the educational process.

By contrast, private institutions often have dress codes that are part of the contract of enrollment. A student who voluntarily enrolls at a private institution is viewed as voluntarily agreeing to the institution's rules, which would include dress codes. Beards, for instance, generally may be prohibited at a private institution, but not at a public institution.

STUDENT ACTIVITY FEES

Student activity fees may be mandatory and used for a variety of purposes, not all of which are agreeable to all students. Student fees voted for student newspapers, student athletic programs, student public interest litigation organizations, and student pro-life or pro-abortion activities have resulted in protests by students who do not wish to provide such funding.

The collection and expenditure of these funds are usually upheld so long as they are not used for purposes that are illegal, noneducational, or supportive of any religion or particular political, economic, social, or personal philosophy, and there is equal access to the funds.

Student organizations with faculty advisors usually may seek some of these funds to aid in supporting their activities. Teachers who serve as advisors to student groups should familiarize themselves with the institution's regulations regarding student activity fees.

Private institutions generally may regulate which student fees are required as long as statutory requirements, such as non-discrimination provisions, are met.

RULES AND REGULATIONS

Specificity

Codes of conduct benefit from being as clear and specific as possible. Try to avoid ambiguity. The general standard in this area is that the degree of specificity required is that which would allow a student to adequately prepare a defense against the charge. Teachers should make plain the prohibited conduct, the procedure for determining whether a student engaged in such conduct, and what the penalty is. Make sure also that the rules are disseminated properly. Finally, assure that the institution follows its own rules.

Disciplinary Rules

Disciplinary rules are those which govern personal behavior of students. They are separate from rules which set forth academic standards, such as degree requirements. Disciplinary rules usually refer to conduct such as alcohol consumption, drug abuse, and parking violations.

EXHAUSTION OF ADMINISTRATIVE REMEDIES

Public institutions may be covered by state administrative procedures acts. These acts may require that a person must exhaust all administrative remedies at the institution before going to court. Generally, a court will not hear a case until all administrative remedies have been exhausted. Thus, a student at a public institution would be required to take a complaint through all internal levels of review at the institution before going outside the institution and filing suit. In the case of a student's being expelled for misconduct, for instance, the student could be required to take the decision from the dean's level to the vice president's level, etc., before being in a position to file a lawsuit in a court.

HANDICAPPED STUDENTS

Section 504 of the Rehabilitation Act of 1973 prohibits discrimination on the basis of handicap. Handicapped students must be "mainstreamed" into academic life as much as possible. However, an institution is not required to so drastically modify or alter an academic program to the extent that the program would be of little or no value to the student completing such a program.

ATHLETICS

Intercollegiate athletic competition is governed by associations such as the National Collegiate Athletic Association and the National Association of Intercollegiate Athletics. Colleges and universities are members of these associations and must adhere to the adopted rules regarding athletic competition.

Athletics at both public and private institutions are affected by federal antidiscrimination statutes. Students cannot be discriminated against in participating in athletics based on race, sex, handicap, or age.

Race is covered by Title VI of the Civil Rights Act of 1964. It requires equal treatment of all races in all federally funded activities. Care should be taken that blacks and whites are counseled equally about achieving their academic goals as well as athletic goals.

Sex discrimination is prohibited by Title IX of the Education Amendments of 1972. Institutions are not required to spend an equal amount of money on men's and women's programs, but are required to accommodate the interests and abilities of students of both sexes. Athletic scholarships should be available in proportionately equal amounts. Separate teams may be fielded for contact sports, such as football, ice hockey, wrestling, boxing, and basketball. Facilities and equipment, as well as coaching, should provide equal opportunity to male and female athletes.

Handicapped students may not be denied the opportunity to participate in athletics solely because of their handicap, according to §504 of the Rehabilitation Act of 1973. Each individual handicapped student should be judged on their own as to whether they are qualified to participate in spite of the handicap. Athletic programs must be accessible to both handicapped student participants and spectators.

Age discrimination is prohibited by the Age Discrimination Act of 1975. However, it is not clear how this act would affect a rule limiting competition for students based upon either a minimum or maximum age.

THE BUCKLEY AMENDMENT

Federal legislation, The Family Educational Rights and Privacy Act of 1974, popularly known as the Buckley Amendment, grants students the right of access to all information placed in their official files. It further provides that only appropriate "school officials" with a "legitimate educational interest" may see students' files without the consent of the student. A log is to be kept listing all persons who view a student's academic record.

Teachers should not post grades unless students give permission to do so and even then it is best that random numbers be assigned so that names and grades cannot be connected.

Personal notes kept by teachers are not subject to students' access rights under the law. However, official grades, etc., kept by the teacher must indeed be available for students to see.

Chapter VI

Employment

LEGAL BASIS OF EMPLOYMENT RELATIONSHIP

The employment relationship between a college teacher and a public institution is based on both constitutional and contract rights. The employment relationship at private institutions is based principally on contract rights. Thus, only faculty at public institutions cannot be punished for exercising their constitutional rights of free expression or free association. For instance, courts have held that faculty at public colleges may not be dismissed for expressing political views, wearing a beard, or not adhering to a recommended dress code. However, private institutions may make rules regarding these matters a part of the employee's contract, and by signing the contract an employee agrees to abide by the rules.

Sometimes a faculty member is hired for an indefinite period of time, and the employment relationship is presumed to be terminable "at-will." Employees hired at-will may be terminated, or choose to leave the position, at any time, with no notice, for any reason or for no reason.

In addition, both public and private institutions generally are covered by federal and/or state statutes prohibiting discrimination in employment based on race, color, national origin, sex, age, marital status, and handicap.

NON-TENURED FACULTY

Non-Renewal

The general rule, except where there is evidence of statutory, contractual, or constitutional rights to the contrary, is that most nontenured faculty have no expectation of continued employment, no right to notice of non-reappointment, no right to a hearing, and no right to reasons for non-reappointment.

De Facto Tenure

Where an institution's rules regarding tenure are written so as to imply continued employment, for example, state that a faculty member should feel that he or she has permanent tenure so long as teaching is satisfactory, attitude is cooperative, and the teacher is happy, a court may find that a de facto tenure contract has been created or that a constitutional interest exists. The faculty member then could be dismissed only for cause, and due process would be required.

Where an institution's rules require notice of non-renewal and no notice is given, a court rarely will find tenure by default. Instead, a court may award money damages.

Stigma

Where there is a constitutional interest or a contractual right, and an accusation is made against a non-tenured faculty member that may place a stigma on the individual's good name or reputation so as to foreclose future employment opportunities, the institution usually is required to provide due process in connection with a non-renewal or dismissal.

TENURED FACULTY

Tenure is awarded to faculty members who meet two sets of criteria. One set of criteria deals with the personal qualifications of the individual. The second set of criteria deals with the needs of the institution. A teacher may be fully qualified personally, but may be refused tenure on the grounds that the institution does not need another tenured person with those qualifications.

Reasons for Dismissal

Four generally recognized causes for dismissal of a tenured faculty member are: professional incompetence, immoral conduct, insubordination or neglect of duty, and the discontinuance or reorganization of a department or a program.

Professional incompetence includes poor teaching or research, not keeping current in one's area of expertise, plagiarism, and offering fraudulent credentials.

Immoral conduct includes making unwelcome sexual advances to students or colleagues.

Insubordination or neglect of duty includes unexplained absences from class, refusal to serve on academic committees, refusal to work with colleagues, and refusal to follow reasonable directions from supervisors.

Discontinuance or reorganization includes decisions by the institution's governing board to eliminate a department, program, or school (such as eliminating a school of nursing, or combining history and political science into one department).

Financial Exigency

A tenured faculty member may be dismissed where an institution demonstrates that a bona fide financial crisis exists. In a financial crisis where there is no provision for layoffs based on seniority, a tenured person may be dismissed and a nontenured person remain where an institution can show that the tenured faculty person's courses are underenrolled and the nontenured person's courses are attracting many students.

Elimination of a Program or Department

In a bona fide financial crisis, an institution may discontinue a department or a program or a whole school. Unless there is institution-wide tenure, rather than the usual departmental tenure, tenured faculty members in the discontinued units may be dismissed. Right to recall or transfer will be determined by the policies of the institution or relevant statutes.

Changing Requirements for Tenure

As the various academic disciplines develop or as an institution grows stronger, the departmental requirements for tenure may change. Persons hired under one set of requirements normally will be expected to meet the new criteria.

Hearing

Notice and hearing should be provided where tenured faculty are being terminated for just cause. In cases of financial exigency, individual tenured faculty may seek to persuade the institution that others, rather than themselves, should be terminated.

LEGAL DISTINCTIONS BETWEEN TENURE AND NON-TENURE

Tenure is not a guarantee of lifetime employment; rather it is a contract providing for continuing employment that can be terminated only for cause. A non-tenure contract differs by virtue of being for a fixed period of time. Thus, both tenure and non-tenure contracts may be terminated for cause during the term of the contract, and such termination would require due process to establish that there was just cause.

Chapter VII

Legal Liability

PERSONAL LIABILITY

Faculty members may be liable personally for certain of their acts. Personal liability could result, for example, where a faculty member deliberately and wrongfully failed a student without sufficient cause; or where a faculty member did not provide appropriate instruction or reasonable supervision in a laboratory and a student was injured. In such instances, a faculty member would be liable personally, and an award of damages could come out of the faculty member's own personal funds.

INSTITUTIONAL LIABILITY

An institution may be liable by itself or together with a faculty member in situations where the faculty member was acting within the scope of employment when the injury occurred. Institutions may be solely liable where there is a breach of the student contract of enrollment, as where courses advertised in the catalogue are not offered, or where students are suspended or expelled for misconduct without proper due process. Institutions may be liable, too, where there is a breach of a faculty member's contract of employment, as when a faculty member is suspended or terminated during the term of the employment contract without due process. Institutions also may be liable for violations of statutes, such as refusing admission on the basis of handicap in violation of the Rehabilitation Act of 1973.

SOVEREIGN OR GOVERNMENTAL OR CHARITABLE IMMUNITY

Public colleges and universities, as governmental agencies, enjoy governmental or sovereign immunity in many states. This immunity may be waived by constitutional provision, statute, or by court decree. Private institutions are not immune from actions in tort unless provided for by law, e.g. given charitable immunity. Individuals, however, are not immune from tort suits irrespective of whether they are employed in public or private institutions and thus they may be sued.

TORT LIABILITY

Definition of a Tort
A tort is a wrongful injury resulting from the breach of a legal duty.

Examples of Torts
Common examples of torts include: negligence, defamation, assault, battery, and false imprisonment.

NEGLIGENCE
Negligence is conduct falling below a prescribed standard for the protection of others.

Elements Necessary to Prove Negligence
Four elements are necessary to prove negligence: the existence of a duty of reasonable care under the circumstances, a breach of the duty, an injury, and a causal relationship between the breach of duty and the injury.

DEFAMATION
Defamation is the tort of holding another person up to hatred, disgrace, ridicule, or contempt.

Libel and Slander
Libel is a false and malicious communication in written form that damages a person's reputation; slander is a similar spoken communication. Truth is usually a defense to accusations of libel and slander.

Teachers should always be on guard about what they say or write about others. For example, a teacher should never accuse a student of cheating in front of a class or where others may hear the accusation. The teacher should try to confront the student in private if possible. Also the teacher should refrain from disparaging remarks about students and others in settings such as teacher lounges, over the bridge table, etc.

Privileged Communications
Certain settings permit privileged communications to take place, even including false statements. An example would be faculty or personnel meetings that are properly called, held in an appropriate setting, carried out in a businesslike fashion, and attended only by persons with a right to be present. These usually are considered to be

privileged settings where people can discuss matters freely without the threat of accusations of defamation. However, if false statements on an irrelevant issue are made in a privileged setting about a person, the privilege may not cover such statements and there may be personal liability.

Faculty should take note that in a discrimination trial where a court ordered a member of a peer review committee to reveal how he voted regarding the promotion of a female and he refused, the committee member was found in contempt of court, fined, and imprisoned briefly.

BASIC DUTIES OF ALL TEACHERS

Act as Reasonable, Prudent Person

Teachers have a duty to act as a reasonable, prudent person under all the circumstances. The more dangerous the situation, the more care should be exercised.

Adequate Supervision

Teachers have a duty to provide adequate supervision. They must supervise their assistants as well as students. Supervision is especially important in gyms and labs and shops. However, a teacher should never feel that there is no responsibility to supervise a class or group for which he or she is responsible.

Proper Instruction

Teachers have a duty to properly instruct how equipment and facilities are to be used. Table saws in theatre shops, for example, require special instruction as to their use. Toxic chemicals require extraordinary precautions. Safety standards should be taught at any time when potential danger is present. For example, the teacher should discuss safety before students conduct an experiment using flammable materials or chemicals.

Maintenance of Equipment and Facilities

Teachers have a duty to see that all equipment and facilities are properly maintained and in good repair. Otherwise, the equipment and facilities should not be used. A teacher may not have to personally repair equipment or facilities, but must report it to the proper authority.

POTENTIAL IS GREAT FOR LAWSUITS

When injury occurs, the injured party generally files suit against both the institution and the particular teacher involved in the incident. The institution has a duty to provide reasonable care, including selecting teachers and others who are properly trained. Certain situations carry more than normal risk of injury and require a higher degree of care on the part of the institution and the teacher.

Laboratories

Chemicals, their noxious fumes, and other dangerous properties cause laboratories to be high risk areas. A teacher is expected to take adequate precautions to see that laboratories are properly maintained and supervised.

Clinical Areas

Some institutions have clinical training involving the treatment of physically and mentally ill patients. Teachers are expected to train carefully the students who work with patients in clinical situations, and also to warn the students of possible dangers both from the patients and from neighborhoods where clinics may be located off campus.

Physical Education Classes

Lawsuits have been filed where students have been injured diving into a shallow part of a pool that was poorly marked, diving into water too deep for their swimming capability, doing gymnastics when the teacher was not there as they jumped off equipment, and wearing the wrong football helmets. Teachers should always take very seriously their responsibilities regarding instruction and supervision. This is especially true in physical education classes.

Shops

Theatre shops are especially risky because student "techies" may not have adequate training to properly run light boards, move scenery, and build sets. Close supervision and adequate instruction is required of all shops.

Intercollegiate and Intramural Sports

Sports activities have resulted in broken and sprained limbs, lost eyes, paralysis, and brain damage. Teachers are expected to monitor sports activity to see that students are placed in the correct levels of play for their experience, age, and weight, and also are expected to make sure that proper safety equipment is worn and maintained. Appropriate medical attention for injuries also should be available.

Student Activities

Teachers assigned to handle student activities are required to exercise care commensurate with the risks attendant to those activities. Dances, parties, and picnics are especially risky due to the possibility of drunkenness and fights, which must be controlled.

Hazing

Hazing is prohibited by law in some states, and is prohibited by campus rules in many instances. There have been a number of deaths and injuries attributed to hazing. In addition to the possible liability of the institution and any teacher assigned to a club accused of hazing, the individual students who caused the hazing injury may be liable, both civilly and criminally.

Field Trips

Field trips carry very high risk. Automobile accidents and airplane crashes have taken their toll of students and faculty on trips. Car drivers and airlines should be selected carefully. Insurance coverage is essential. Institutional guidelines for field trips should be established and followed with no deviations.

Waivers

Waivers of liability often are not effective because they are found to be against public policy. Responsibility releases may be effective. In some instances, injured parties have been found to have assumed the risk of what they are doing. However, only normal risks can be assumed, not risks that amount to gross negligence. Thus, one may assume the risk of injury from normal body contact in a football game, but not the risk of injury from falling into an unmarked open pit alongside the field where new drainage pipes are being installed.

ALCOHOL

The liability connected to the use of alcohol has expanded with the passage of legislation, as well as court decisions, in some states that makes both vendors and social hosts liable if they permit persons having too much to drink to operate motor vehicles and an injury results. This statutory third party liability provides victims of drunk drivers with a remedy for injuries. In addition, liability may exist on the basis of negligence in situations where drunken persons injure others or themselves.

Teachers who have responsibility for any activity where alcohol is present must make certain that all state laws and regulations are observed. Identification must be checked so that no minor is served alcohol.

DEFENSES AGAINST TORT ACTIONS

Assumption of the Risk

Assumption of the risk is a defense to a tort action. That is, the injured party is deemed to have assumed the risk when he or she engaged in the activity. Assumption of the risk is a good defense where the injury was due to the normal risks of a situation, but not if due to abnormal risks. Thus, a student participating in diving would be expected to assume the normal risks associated with diving, but would not be expected to assume a risk such as negligently superheated water that caused severe burns.

Contributory Negligence

Contributory negligence is a defense to a tort action. That is, the injured party's own negligence contributed to the injury. A boxer who removed his mouth guard without his coach's knowledge could not allege successfully that his mouth injury was due to the negligence of the coach or the institution.

Act of God

A tort suit may be defended by showing that the direct cause of the injury was, in fact, an Act of God, such as a flood, a blizzard, or a bolt of lightning, over which the institution or teacher had no control.

Statutory Limitations

Tort suits must be filed within a statutory time limit, such as two, three or five years. Where a suit has been filed too late, usually the injured party has lost the opportunity for redress.

PRIVILEGED COMMUNICATIONS

A qualified immunity protects communications made by a person having a particular duty to another person having a corresponding duty. An example would be communications necessary to the functioning of a personnel committee.

Letters of Recommendation

A letter of recommendation concerning a candidate for a position, or a student applying for graduate school, may be a privileged communication if it is written by a person requested to supply it, addressed to a person authorized to request it, speaks only about matters related to job qualifications, and is not circulated beyond the committee. False information contained in such a letter would not generally be grounds for a tort suit, unless it could be shown that the falsity of the information was known to the writer and put forth maliciously. The qualified privilege extends only to properly called meetings held in a businesslike manner, not to informal phone calls or golf course gossiping.

When in doubt, do not agree to write letters of recommendation.

Breaking Confidentiality

Teachers should understand that sometimes confidences must be broken or the teacher may be liable for negligent conduct causing an injury. For example, teachers and counselors are expected to inform parents or proper authorities where a student seriously threatens suicide. Where a student seriously threatens to kill or harm a named victim, there is a duty to notify the intended victim.

Serving on a Tenure and Promotion Committee

Ordinarily, deliberations by members of a tenure and promotion committee are to be kept confidential. However, where a court orders members of such a committee to reveal its votes, as in an employment discrimination case, the members must reveal their votes or face a finding of contempt of court which may lead to a fine and imprisonment.

CIVIL RIGHTS LIABILITY UNDER 42 U.S.C. §1983

Teachers at public institutions usually are considered to be state officials. The Civil Rights Act of 1871, known as 42 U.S.C. §1983, prohibits the denial of constitutional or statutory rights by public officials. Where teachers deprive students of their rights under the Constitution and laws, the students may file suit under 42 U.S.C. §1983. Similarly, where public institutions deprive teachers or administrators of similar rights, the teachers or administrators may file suit. Usually the suit is filed against both the public institutions and the teachers or administrators involved. The teachers or administrators may be found personally liable.

Attorney's Fees

The prevailing party in a suit filed under federal civil rights laws generally is entitled to attorney's fees.

SEXUAL HARASSMENT

Sexual harassment is defined as unwelcome sexual advances, requests for sexual favors, or verbal or physical conduct of a sexual nature. Examples include: unwelcome hugging, kissing, or touching, as well as promising good grades or a job promotion in exchange for a date or sexual favor.

Sexual harassment may involve males and females, males and males, or females and females.

Sexual harassment of students is prohibited by Title IX of the Education Amendments of 1972. Sexual harassment of employees and colleagues is prohibited by Title VII of the Civil Rights Act of 1964. In addition, other civil and criminal charges may be pressed.

Faculty members should avoid any conduct that could be interpreted as an unwelcome sexual advance by a student or a colleague.

LIABILITY INSURANCE

Coverage for Institution

An institution should seek the advice or both an attorney and an insurance agent regarding the kinds of risks the institution and its employees and students face and the kinds of insurance available to cover them. Public institutions need to be aware of civil rights liability, and try to find insurance that will include that coverage.

Some institutions have become self-insurers, setting aside a pool of funds for insurance purposes.

Employees acting within the scope of their employment usually are indemnified by their employer for any awards against them. An employee's defense costs also may be covered by the institution's insurance.

Coverage by Individual

In addition to any insurance or indemnification provided by an institution, every faculty member should have individual personal liability insurance. This is necessary to cover situations where an institution may allege that a faculty member who is being sued was acting outside the scope of employment and therefore the institution cannot provide a defense or indemnification.

Chapter VIII

Risk Management

MINIMIZING RISKS

Individual faculty members, as well as institutions, would benefit from managing their professional lives so as to minimize risks. One way to do this is to take a preventive law stance in the classroom and in all other dealings with students and colleagues.

STANDARDS OF THE PROFESSION

In the Classroom

Make sure that all degree requirements are understood by students, that all courses are accurately described, that all course syllabi are up to date, that lecture notes are kept current, and that grading is done fairly and in a timely fashion.

Safety standards for labs, physical education, and shops should be clear and made known to students by posting or handing out copies and discussing the standards with the students.

Outside the Classroom

Meetings to advise students, or the holding of office hours, should be done in an open and businesslike fashion. Faculty need to be available to students, but would be wise to hold all meetings in offices on campus. Social events at residences or similar off-campus sites attended by faculty and students can be quite beneficial, but should be conducted in a manner that maintains an arm's length atmosphere. It would be better not to have a social event than have one that places parties in legal jeopardy.

KEEPING ABREAST OF CURRENT LEGAL PARAMETERS

Publications

Faculty members would do well to read widely and stay abreast of developments in their own fields as a way of improving and maintaining their competence in their fields. In addition, it is important to read publications that summarize trends and developments regarding legal issues in higher education.

Seminars

Faculty members also should take every advantage provided for attendance at seminars and other meetings where their disciplinary interests are discussed. Seminars and meetings that explain new developments in legal issues also are of value.

RESPECTING RIGHTS OF STUDENTS, ADMINISTRATORS, OTHER FACULTY AND STAFF

When in doubt as to what to do, and no one is around to ask, follow the Golden Rule—Do Unto Others As You Would Have Others Do Unto You.

Chapter IX

Checklist for College Teachers Regarding Legal Issues

ACADEMIC AND STUDENT CONDUCT ISSUES

1. Are you familiar with the college's requirements for receiving a degree, as set forth in the college catalogue, the policies of the governing board, the student handbook, departmental rules, and any other pertinent document?

2. Do you treat alleged plagiarism and cheating as a serious disciplinary matter which involves the reputation of the student?

3. Are you clear about when due process regarding academic and student conduct issues is required at your institution, and what that process is?

4. Do you know the penalties students may suffer for violations of academic or behavior standards?

5. Do you know what review procedures are available regarding adverse decisions about violations of academic or behavior standards?

6. Do you have an up to date syllabus for each of the courses you are teaching, that includes an outline of the course, requirements for class attendance, required reading, grading criteria, and office hours?

7. Do you make special efforts to stay current in your field of expertise?

8. Are you careful about conducting your classes in a non-discriminatory manner?

9. Are you careful about avoiding conduct with students that could be interpreted as sexual harassment?

10. Do you exercise reasonable care regarding the safety of your students in class, labs and shops?

11. Are you familiar with your college's policies and procedures regarding field trips?
12. Do you take adequate precautions in planning and conducting field trips?
13. If students or others in your class become disruptive, do you know when and how to call campus security?

EMPLOYMENT ISSUES

1. Do you understand your employment relationship to your institution, e.g., whether you are employed under a contract, at-will, on a tenure track or not, have tenure or not?
2. Do you have a copy of the college's employment policies as stated in the governing board policies, the faculty handbook, departmental personnel rules, and other pertinent documents, regarding promotions, salary increases, tenure, leaves of absence, holidays, vacations, retirement benefits?
3. Are you clear about what your employment responsibilities are regarding teaching, research, service?
4. Do you keep current in your field?
5. Do you present papers at meetings, publish articles, seek research funds, supervise graduate students, and give other evidence of being active in your field?
6. Do you take your turn serving on institutional and departmental committees?
7. When serving on a personnel committee, are you careful to make judgments based on candidates' qualifications as they relate to your department's job descriptions so that allegations of discrimination are not substantiated?
8. Do you make every effort to work harmoniously with colleagues, superiors, staff, and students?
9. Do you meet your classroom teaching responsibilities diligently, presenting good, solid lectures, being on time to class, maintaining a good learning environment, keeping office hours as set, grading according to set criteria and in a timely fashion, and avoiding any discriminatory conduct?
10. Do you provide a good role model for students and younger colleagues, e.g., stressing responsible scholarship, academic freedom, appropriate attribution when work of students or other scholars is used, rigorous research methods, proper disclosure of research and noting corrections when errors are made?
11. If you are seeking tenure, are you clear about what your department expects successful candidates to demonstrate regarding qualifications? Do you have a mentor?

36

Chapter X

Pertinent Federal Statutes—In Brief

TEACHING

Statute	Purpose	Implications	Enforcement / Information
Age Discrimination Act of 1975	Prohibits discrimination on the basis of age by recipients of federal assistance.	Admission and treatment of mature students.	Enforced by individual federal agencies.
Copyright Act (1980)	Limits use of copyrighted material, such as literary works (including computer programs and videocassette recordings), music, drama, and dance for teaching and library purposes.	Making copies for classroom or personal use.	Register of Copyrights, Library of Congress.
Title IX, Education Amendments of 1972	Prohibits sex discrimination in all education programs and activities that receive federal assistance.	Treatment of female students regarding admission, financial aid, academics, and athletics.	U.S. Department of Education.

Statute	Purpose	Implications	Enforcement / Information
Family Educational Rights and Privacy Act of 1974 (Buckley Amendment)	Provides criteria for access by students and parents to students' academic records, and requires consent of student or parent to release such information to others.	Confidentiality of academic records.	U.S. Department of Education.
Human Subjects Research Regulations (1974)	Protects rights of human subjects "at risk" in experiments, demonstration projects, teaching programs, or evaluations.	Notification of possible risks and informed consent prior to subjects' participation in experiments.	U.S. Department of Health and Human Services.

EMPLOYMENT

Statute	Purpose	Implications	Enforcement / Information
Age Discrimination in Employment Act of 1967	Prohibits discrimination in employment against persons between ages 40 and 70.	Hiring and promotions on basis of job qualifications rather than age.	U.S. Equal Employment Opportunity Commission.
Title VII Civil Rights Act of 1964	Prohibits employment discrimination based on race, color, religion, sex, national origin.	Discriminatory hiring, promotions, or terminations.	U.S. Equal Employment Opportunity Commission.
Equal Pay Act of 1963	Requires females and males receive equal pay for equal work.	Lower rank or salary for female than male holding teaching position requiring equal skill, effort, and responsibility, and performed under similar working conditions.	U.S. Equal Employment Opportunity Commission.

Statute	Purpose	Implications	Enforcement / Information
Occupational Safety & Health Act of 1970	Sets safety & health standards in places of employment.	Proper ventilation and other safety standards.	U.S. Department of Labor (or state labor department).
Vietnam Era Veterans' Readjustment Assistance Act of 1974	Provides equal employment opportunity for Vietnam era veterans.	Refusal to make reasonable accommodation to physical or mental limitations of Vietnam veterans.	U.S. Department of Labor.

GENERAL

Statute	Purpose	Implications	Enforcement / Information
Civil Rights Act of 1866, 42 U.S.C. §1981	Prohibits racial discrimination in making and enforcing contracts.	Refusal to contract to admit to facilities or programs or employment because of race.	Suit for damages or equitable relief in either federal or state court. Personal liability is possible.
Civil Rights Act of 1871, 42 U.S.C. §1983	Prohibits denial of constitutional and statutory rights by public officials.	Deprivation by public official of property interest (employment or attendance at public college) or liberty interest (good name or reputation).	Suit for damages or equitable relief in either federal or state court. Personal liability is possible.
Title VI, Civil Rights Act of 1984	Prohibits racial or ethnic discrimination in educational institutions receiving federal aid.	Refusal to supply instruction in English to substantial groups of non-English-speaking students.	U.S. Departments of Education, and Health and Human Services.
Sunshine Acts	Require public decision making to be done in open meetings and public records to be open to public scrutiny.	Refusal of board of trustees of public college to admit public to meetings.	Suit in federal or state court.

Statute	Purpose	Implications	Enforcement / Information
Rehabilitation Act of 1973	Prohibits discrimination against handicapped persons in education and employment.	Refusal to admit handicapped person as student solely on basis of handicap in spite of academic qualifications; or to hire handicapped person in spite of job qualifications.	U.S. Departments of Education and Labor.

Resources for Legal Information in Secondary and Higher Education

If you have found the information contained in this monograph to be helpful in your day-to-day operations and as a reference it is quite likely that you may also be interested in other titles included in the *The Higher Education Administration Series* or in our publications that offer quarterly updates on case law related to various fields of education.

Following is a list of titles available from College Administration Publications. Where the titles are not illustrative of the subject covered, a brief description is included. If you wish to order, there is an order blank on the reverse side of this sheet which you may wish to copy rather than tearing out this page.

Other titles in *The Higher Education Administration Series*:
- ▶ Administering College and University Housing:
  A Legal Perspective
- ▶ The Dismissal of Students with Mental Disorders:
  Legal Issues, Policy Considerations
  and Alternative Responses

The following publications offer the reader a quarterly report on recent precedent setting higher court decisions covering a wide range of subjects in the area encompassed by the self-descriptive title. In addition, through the accumulated back issues, and in the "College" publications, a casebook, each of these publications are also excellent comprehensive references that can be of great help in day-to-day operations and long range planning:
- ▶ The College Student and the Courts
- ▶ The College Administrator and the Courts
- ▶ The Schools and the Courts

While primarily written for practicing administrators, superintendents, school boards, teachers and legal counsel in secondary education, this publication is of great value to related schools of education.

Order Blank

Bill to:............................ Ship to:............................

....

....

Quantity	Item	Price	Total
_____	The Dismissal of Students with Mental Disorders:		_____
	One to nine copies @ $9.95		
	Ten or more copies @ $9.50		
_____	Administering College and University Housing:		_____
	One to nine copies @ $9.95		
	Ten or more copies @ $9.50		
_____	A Practical Guide to Legal Issues Affecting College Teachers		_____
	One to nine copies @ $4.95		
	Ten to twenty-four copies @ $3.95		
	Twenty-five or more copies @ $3.50		
_____	The College Student and the Courts Includes casebook, all back issues and four quarterly updating supplements	$87.50	_____
_____	The College Administrator and the Courts Includes casebook, all back issues and four quarterly updating supplements	$77.50	_____
_____	The Schools and the Courts Includes over 600 pages of back issues and four updating reports	$67.50	_____
	Postage (if payment accompanies order we will ship postpaid)		_____
	North Carolina residents add appropriate sales tax		_____
	Total		_____

Address Orders to:
College Administration Publications, Inc.
Dept. LG, P.O. Box 8492, Asheville, NC 28814

☐ Pricing of the above publications was correct on the publication date of this monograph. If you wish to be advised of current prices of titles you have ordered before shipment, please check.

☐ For further information regarding any of the above titles please indicate with check here and in the quantity column of each publication and we will forward current brochures and current order information.